# Whale Language:
# Songs Of Iona

# Angela Locke

## Indigo Dreams Publishing

First Edition: Whale Language: Songs Of Iona
First published in Great Britain in 2011 by:
Indigo Dreams Publishing
132 Hinckley Road
Stoney Stanton
Leics
LE9 4LN

www.indigodreams.co.uk

Angela Locke has asserted her right under the Copyright, Designs
and Patents Act 1988 to be identified as the author of this work.
©2011 Angela Locke

ISBN 978-1-907401-50-3

British Library Cataloguing in Publication Data. A CIP record for
this book can be obtained from the British Library.

Designed and typeset in Palatino Linotype by Indigo Dreams.

Cover design by Ronnie Goodyer at Indigo Dreams
Author photo by Stephen Goodwin

Printed and bound in Great Britain by Imprint Academic, Exeter.

Papers used by Indigo Dreams are recyclable products made from
wood grown in sustainable forests following the guidance of the
Forest Stewardship Council.

I would like to dedicate these poems to my three beautiful daughters, and to my beloved grandchildren, those who are already in the world, and those who are yet to come. They have brought me so much joy, and I wish them great joy in return and many blessings in their inheritance of this precious Earth.

I would also like to send love and many thanks to the amazing writers who have worked with me on my Iona Writing Retreats over the last 10 years. They have poured so much creative energy into their wonderful work, and it will always live with me as an evocation of that magical island.

Special thanks are due to all the wonderful staff of the Argyll Hotel on Iona, including Claire and Dan, the owners, and Jann, the Manager. You have all given me so much support over the years of running my Writing Retreats and made us all so welcome. Thank you too to the islanders of Iona who have shown me so much hospitality and kindness. There are strong connections between Iona and New Zealand, as some families emigrated there after the clearances. I would like to extend grateful thanks to the New Zealanders who made me so welcome. The people of Christchurch NZ are especially in my thoughts at the moment after the devastating earthquake. A special thank you is due to Graham and Linda Mackenzie who invited us to stay in their wonderful 'Sea House' in Hahei, NZ. Also to the Maori of Christchurch and Kaikoura who gave me such insight into tribal life, and lastly to the Tibetan people for their wisdom and humour in the face of adversity.

I would like to thank my assistants Sue Catterson and Norma Gunn for their hard work in deciphering my notebooks and, last but not least, my husband Colin who is, as ever, a tower of strength in times of need, wherever I am in the world.

The haunting language of whales seems to speak of a profound planetary wisdom which, on some level, we may feel we understand. Some whale species may be the oldest mammals on Earth, and whales, with their huge brains, can communicate over hundreds, possibly thousands of miles with their complex songs. If they have wisdom we cannot yet comprehend, it must be deep indeed. They cause no harm to our precious planet. They sing to one another in the depths of the oceans, they are mammals like us, and yet their ancient songs are threatened by human despoliation of our only home, the home we share.

Whale experts are concerned that noise pollution in the oceans is shutting down the whales' long-distance communication systems. To me, this seems a paradigm for our own fragile state as we cling, increasingly disorientated, to our beautiful planet. Our understanding of the sacred, our deep awareness of the mystical power of Earth, our tribal wisdom, is threatened by the busyness of our lives, the 'white noise', the stress, the pollution. In these poems I am trying, in my own inadequate language, to express some of what we do not have words *for*, something that may be lost, some *otherness* we need to honour, to celebrate and to protect. It is that 'ghostly language of the ancient earth' which Wordsworth understood so well, which the Druids celebrated on sacred Iona, which the Maori inhabit in their *marae*, which the Tibetans enshrine every day in their sacred rituals, which native peoples everywhere still have 'whale language' *for*. It is that still spirit, the *numinous*, which links us to the mystery of Life.

Angela Locke
Cumbria 2011

# CONTENTS

# Whale Language: Songs Of Iona

# Whales off the North beach:  Iona

Companionably, quietly
They come together in blue water,
Black, glossy tails glinting in sunlight.
Unhurried, exactly equidistant,
They stroll the sea beyond the black rocks,
Where surf threshes the edges of land.
Even across the distance of the bay
I hear them, their inaudible
Whale language.
Their presence fills the bay with silence
And deep speech.
I am drawn into the circle of their being,
Aware of stillness,
Creation weaving its web,
The rub of particle and molecule
Between sea and land,
The endless sexual game of thee and me
Between edges, and frontiers, the journeys between,
The journey the sea makes, its language,
How we share its tides in our gut,
How these black-tailed whales sing our songs,
Dance our dance.

We wave to one another
In our steady progress,
Me in the hayfield above the machair,
They in their own place,
Effortlessly, peacefully
Cutting diamond water, while
simultaneously ruminating on the state of the world,
and rewriting Hamlet for whales.

## Nada Brahma

*Nada brahma* – the world is sound.
The rock vibrates, singing its own song,
that song of Iona, the song of ancient things,
of beginnings, when rock cooled,
before fossils were laid down,
before there was time for death.


No watchers in the cauldron saw the planet boil and cool,
No one saw green rock emerge from the cave of the sea,
coalescing as islands. No-one but God,
singing the world into existence.
*Nada brahma, nada brahma*
Life came into its place.  Fish swam and crawled.
At last we came, on our own pilgrimage,
looking for the first line of the song.

## IOna

jewel in Earth's stone
set in the sea's ring
you touch the skin of the world
like a birthstone
      held in that memory of Birth
back when the elemental beingness
      of creation
      seemed simple enough
         for understanding
remembering what we knew
         holding the Universe
         in the palm of our
            hands

## Beginning

We are each, alone, that creative flame.
At the head of the valley is the shadow of the rock.
The flame burns under a juniper tree,
in the snow white mountain in a secret cave,
in the quiet source of the river, in light on water,
the first leaf, darkness and sleep.


All burns to that creative life
we reflect within us,
that flame the precious ounce of azurite,
the luminous light of the soul,
the infinite universe, the point of no thing,
 where we may begin.

# Sea House, Hahei, New Zealand

An ounce of azurite will do it. Michelangelo knew
what put divinity into a painting,
what gave it back to God; the Madonna's robe
gleaming with the light of blue angels,
an ounce of more-than-gold, painting
the sea's perfection. This oyster of a bay,
green-lipped, has a pearl set
within its curve; a peak of carved wood,
a house rearing proud as a ship,
listening long to the heartbeat of the sea.

Ancestors have landed in this place,
put a hand on a map and said: This will be
our coming home, our *marae*. Children and grandchildren
will grow in this good place. They will dream of it
when they are away, this sea house shining in the bay,
dream of laughter and the sea's whisper.
A poem of the sea will come into their minds
like a slow joy, and they will remember how they woke
in early dawns and heard the sea's thrum, and knew
they had come home.

## Seals on the Island of Women: Sound of Iona

The seals lie by the great ocean
And on the wind I hear their singing;
A door creaking in the silence,
An abandoned pup,
The wild cry of a lost soul.

Something draws us in. That siren song,
If heard alone on a wild night,
Would tear your heart,
Call you out into the dark.

## Sacred Iona

Beside the turquoise always turning sea
I find my peace
shining shells buried in halfmade sand
gulls calling among ruined churches
old stones bearing a pattern of the past

every corner holds secrets
I draw breath in a honey-coloured room
someone else will make my bed
thank god I'm tired
just now walk the long road more slowly till I stop

breathe the long breath
more slowly   the island calling
I hardly sleep   don't need to
heart opening like a morning daisy
simple   till I'm cut down

I lie at night breathing stars
lap of water on a white shore
black rocks   walk a path of early ritual
boats going out to fish
those quiet sounds of morning

caught in a net of light
I only need to hold my hand
against the heart's land
to feel its beat
its life

# Sun in the Nunnery Gardens : Iona

All growing things are transformed by light.
Spears of flags, grass, the hedge, the shine on bluebell
leaves;
moss on ruins, hart's tongue fern licking like a slow cat
from crevices.
It's wicked, the way it snakes into the light;
Venus flytraps for the sun.
Here Iona's stone, stacked in blocks,
tied to earth, still sings of the sea, aeons of time
before the angels came.

# Dandelion Rock

More sun flowers than Van Gogh's, this burst of yellow gold
explodes in air like frozen energy. Yet it's an illusion.
Every particle is held for a moment in the sunburst,
seeking to spread into the world. These clocks,
throwing out Time into the wind, are unstable as electrons,
any movement of air sending seed into the sky,
dandelionating the world, seedheads left behind, a button
of skin pricked with pores, while hairs are held
silk-globed, sepals flattened backwards
like a running greyhound, a rocket streaming into space,
free at last of Earth. Framed by spear-like leaves,
it's on the move. We see its evolution as it passes through
Alpha Centauri, floating light years on the solar wind.

This rock meanwhile is going nowhere. Hard-landscaped
in a shifting world, atoms hold hands tightly -
yet not so tightly that the sea, the sun, the wind can't get in
there,
working away for change, grinding down the shell,
fingering away at rock, finding crevices, turning quartz,
green marble, calcium from old bones, back to Earth.
It takes time to unlock those hands, full of prejudices
about who they are, something solid in an ephemeral world,
yet grind down green glass and it makes a garden in the
end.

And all the while, this sun clock is ticking Time away,
exploding the myth of ephemera, with silk dancing
on the wind, dancing, dancing towards immortality.

## After the Hurricane

All that slow growth and memory of trees is gone.
We retile roofs, mend broken fences,
while insurance claims for chimneys
blip slowly through computers.

But no one can mend the trees;
neither faith healers nor tree surgeons
can knit these bones together,
nor fit my trees back into these open scars.

They lie along the ground, huge roots
clodded with earth, as though the wrenched wood
clings to what has gone, and under each,
a small clearness, craters filled with rain.

A little sky here, and mirrored water,
and now the sun which once could only weevil its way
into the dark, can paint earth with light,
and plants will come which have laid sleeping until now.

Looking down and down we see shadows of nested roots
deep under, like imprints of a Viking burial.
We feel the strange obscenity of looking
into earth, which once was secret.

The wood's heart is shuttered by fallen trees,
and no surgeon's saw will free it;
yet fox and badger will play in spaces
which the moon discovers, without fear.

Perhaps the wood, wounded almost to death,
has broken free.

## Iona : Easter

A rainbow beside the abbey
links land and sky, island and mainland,
where houses left behind glow white
against a rainrinsed sky

Turquoise water and white sand
draw into one other, separated,
yet conjoined by rock.
The abbey stands in a plain space
plainsong, stone, arch,
solidly upon the earth.

Something lifts us
as the soughing wind
creeps under old doors
with a wild cry to the heart.
We think of doves in the morning
as streamers of Easter tassels
stir in that old breeze

Across the Sound,
the ferry cries as it beaches
like an old whale
who has lost her calf.

# Yoga with Eucalyptus blossom : Australia

Our daughter, brown as a fawn,
Steps alone into sunlight on the veranda.
Long-limbed and cool, utterly herself,
She is caught in her own stillness,
A point of balance which is pure grace.

An old dress flows from her, as she carries
Eucalyptus blossom, honey-scented,
In an earthen jug. A gift
To the green garden.

# Kintra, Mull : Tides After the Clearances

A silent waiting of mud and kelp
as the sea creeps. This melancholy creature
has seen old wives gather on the shore,
heard how they keen when tides do not keep promises;
all those old griefs – peat smoke at dusk from chimneys,
children huddled on the earth floor, that slow floodtide,
edging through sullen channels, wet-lipped
as it mouths the edges of stones.

The retreat is sounded somewhere
on the moon; shy, regretful, silent, without wave or current.
All sorrows in this land are leached out
on the ebb, as slow tears in another watcher's past.

# Himalayan Rainbow

we meet on the bridge between us
a rainbow arches over the valley
between mountain and mountain
this is the bridge
everything beneath is changed

we are linked for ever by this
the rainbow bridge
great mountains where the gods live
a cherry tree lit by the morning sun

# Iona: North Wind in Spring

Blonde bleached reeds comb the ditch.
Brittle, flagged with ancient seed,
they bend backwards in the wind.
An iridescent sea, turquoise-skimmed, echoes
in the neck feathers of two pigeons in the field.

The North Wind, light-bringer, colour painter.
*The North wind doth blow and we shall have snow.*
But it's spring! In the pasture two dark lambs nuzzle,
necks entwined, nose to tail. Out in the bay,
towards the Paps of Jura, a collar of foam lifts and falls
around rocks.That cunning cuckoo hasn't arrived;
too soon to disguise herself in lush Maytime foliage.
Only the corncrake gives voice to his harsh burr,
as gannets mount and mount the wind,
hurling arrowed bodies into the wild sea.

*May the wind be always at your back!*
A Celtic blessing if ever there was one.
But would you go on and on walking with the wind,
and never turn for home?

## The Young Violinist

Music is the spiritual map:
In the stratosphere, sometimes,
Arching in a parabola
It touches pure spirit.

The girl is tangled in the autumn trees,
A few yellow leaves, the rain at dusk;
Shadows of us beyond the window
And the girl playing, warm as peaches,
Summer in our hands.
She takes us back to joy.

Closing my eyes, I see that sound
Mellow on the inner dark, so round
And touchable. I reach myself to it,
Caught in sadness and delight, as music is,
And still she floats beyond the window
In the autumn tree.

An abandoned ball lies in the orchard.
The girl, playing her violin
As though her body depended on it,
Catches us between the worlds

Of longing, memory, sadness.
There, beyond the window
Is the tipsy lamp; a grand piano
Held open with encyclopaedias.
A fan case, clock, blue china in a cabinet.
She catches us, tells us what we are
In that yellow light. Then reaching up
With white hands, she plucks the afternoon,
The rain, sadness in the autumn grass,
And throws it.

## Alder Tree

With the heart's eye, the ancient wisdom sees
the sprite, the dryad; knows that energy
translates into matter – and back again.
Long before Einstein, the Old Ones knew
invisible beings inhabit the edges;
this leaf, a manifestation of energy drawn
as greenery from the tree, imagined in its perfection.
Sketched to a plan, it lies in the bud until unfurled.
Is there a shadow form behind this near-perfection,
the Angel of the Alder tree drawing the plan
for this fine filigree, this pale green,
these cones dancing against the blue?

# Findhorn Light

The simple loveliness of things,
Jade green sea against a darkened sky,
White flashing wings above the sun,
Where waves are surfed with white.

The tide ebbs, leaving light-filled space.
Pools, roughened by the wind's kiss,
Glitter. Herring gulls dip beaks in light,
The old world turns.

Walk this blinding path,
This lacewing light,
woven into oystercatcher call.

Diamond light which cups and holds
This bay, this blue, this universe of fluid sand,
These eggs of stones held in the wind's hiss,
Stained glass windowed seaweed flagging the sea.

From this chalice of our inner life,
We spill the fluid world into existence,
Dream the dreams, spin this light
In webs to catch us back

# Fête Day: Bay of Mont St. Michel

Here is a woman with stars in her dress,
a white dress blowing across white sand,
turquoise sea, the possibility of dolphins,
a fishing boat, painted red, on this painted ocean.

What is the plan?
The plan is three white butterflies
will invent geometry in this white world,
houses will dream behind shutters.

At midday on the *jour de fête*, laughter will return.
The red boat will be untied.
Like a balloon, it will bob across this great bay
to an unknown destination.

Angels, said to inhabit this place
in a timeless present, have approved this crimson boat
setting out to catch grey mullet,
forever dancing on the tide.

Look! The sea moon has become that red-boated balloon,
bouncing round a darkening world,
talking to sleeping butterflies and angels.

## Walking to Pokhara

Moon is in the peepal tree
      the boatman slaps the rope
each time it lifts
     it falls
a glittering curve of light

the world is candlelit tonight
    the whole of life is centred down
to light on faces
    glow of copper pans

    in open-fronted rooms
old men sit and smile
    the prayer wheels turn

and while the candles burn
    moths in the flame
we draw closer than we dared
    in the mighty world
each face is lit
    for us alone

light is on the water, spreading
    and where a candle is,
a life blooms
    we would not see
in darkness

## Outside In

You are outside, in the dusk,
Watching the lighted window;
A table laid for supper,
The busyness of other lives
Seeming perfect. The frost falls so swiftly
Your lips crack with it,
The fells so clear they ring.
You want to be here
In the almost dark,
To hold the last gold light
Touching the summit,
To know you are alone.
Yet that light beyond the window
Is lit and now curtains are drawn
Against that night you are part of,
And you are outside.

## Om shanti

I hold you in the flower of my Being
in my heart centre
a place of infinite Light
of infinite possibility
a blue iris
opening with a golden centre

here is the flame
nothing can extinguish
my sense of infinite self
of infinite non-self

it is the Quaker silence
the Om Shanti
the magnolia tree
in the courtyard

wings of eagles
in the silence
emptiness filled with Light

this blue eternal flower
it is who I am
it is who I am, unforgotten

only needing to return
to my centre
to remember

## Across the Water

Across the water the sound of a pipe
calls me home. Land born, rooted in the growing earth,
I am standing now on the edge of the firm world.
My feet, flattened in sand, make my mark,
small waves lap my feet, tugging me in.
The sea sucks earth away to new places,
the long drag of it, shingle scours the beach,
polishing, changing, shifting, renewing,
undermining the solid edges of a world I thought I knew.

Now the piper's call from the distant isle draws closer.
I stand still, on the last line of the land.

## Peace : Iona

Oh for that scallop shell of quiet!
Is there a place where Life,
That old adversary, retreats a little
And in the silence makes a truce
With me?  The tranquil sea
At first light when the boats go out to fish,
The early song of blackbirds in the apple tree,
The hush of evening, late sun through beech trees,
Owl call under the sliver of a winter moon,
My own night bed, warm under the duvet.

Just for a little while, just now,
Life retreats, is merciful.
There's nothing left to do
But sleep.

# Tai Chi in the nunnery garden: Iona

Waving hands like the Clouds,
I am Iona air, fresh as the sea's breath.
I move among bluebells and wallflowers
in the nunnery garden, and  remind myself
I must not interfere. I am the element
which floats above and moves among,
neither touching nor changing
simply the unengaged observer.
This is hard for me.
I see that tulip needs rearranging, that weed,
that bird coming closer, trusting, asking for food.
It is hard to become my hands
sighing through the element of Air,
to know this is the way to be,
simply as clouds pass over the sun into empty sky,
my consciousness making no difference in the world.
And next, I am glad of Fire which wakes me
as hot tea does at home. I swing my arms and punch,
feeling the fire dragon fly along my spine
enthusing me, quicksilver, flame along the ground of being.
And water, as waves on the shore,
I celebrate their holding back, their falling,
their intimate relationship with stone and sand,
how they drag, hold and change,
smoothing pebbles, interleaving sand granules
with water, a soup of living beach.

Then I am the shell pool, my fingers touching silk,
That well of eternal youth on Dun I, mysterious depths,
unexplained ripples. I am this circle of dark possibility,
then lifting drops, become a rainbow, then fire dragon
again, perfect strength and power.
Marking my body's chakras,
I walk down, from crown to base, seeing dew on grass,
seeing the air move flowers. I blow through window spaces
in the chancel, as gulls scream and lift above their empty eyes,
spaces against sky.
I see fire has marked the stone, some ancient flame,
the sacking by Vikings or Danes.
I place my hands on Earth,
feeling the depth of the planet.
All is change, all the same.

# Myth

*'We are from the beginning of creation*
*Without old age, without consummation of earth.'*
    The Voyage of Bran: early Irish text

Rhiannon of the white waterfall
waits    combing her spray hair

high in the rowan tree which
overhangs the pool of her being
wind calls the mountain home

wind lifts the spray
night falls
Rhiannon waits

with the coming of the first star
wind changes    frost breathes on grass
owl calls

softer than footfall
an air of magic
rings in the bell of the night

breathes on Rhiannon's white hair
binding it to stillness
now when the wind blows

her hair chimes like a faery clock
she is mouth-open in a spell
the knife of the old dark

pierces her frozen heart
the cord of Earth is cut
again
again
     again

# Crows at the Feast

Then in the early morning the crows came,
flying low across the sea,
there at the tide before the seagulls.

The seagulls were too busy, perched on chimneypots,
each one higher than the last,
from the moment the sun struck the chimneypots,
shouting, waking the residents of the village,
screaming that they alone were kings of the castle.

Down on the beach, low tide.
Crows, who had learned from ancestors
how to pick up shellfish in their beaks,
lifted themselves on black wings,
dashing shells onto dark rocks,
gobbling the raw cockles.

By the time the gulls, yelling fury,
came whitely onto the weed-strewn beach
the crows were off to some other destination.

The tide crept in, slowly, slowly,
covering the shellfish in their half-life.
The time of feasting was past.
Some had been wiser than others.

## Seahorses

I am looking into water
Searching for the wild seahorses
Will they be singing?
Will they be drowning?

My eyes are under the waves
The world is strangely blue

I am looking into water
Searching for the wild seahorses
Will they be singing?
Will they be drowning?

This world
Is a bowl of blue hyacinths
Caught in the sun

## Earth Music

Music is the breathing of the Earth
made Sound

the manifest Sound
of all unsounded things

light flickering on willow
damp woods
the mushroom touch of skin
lemondrop taste of windfall pears

even sounded things
taken beyond their sound
are in this music

sighing trees in night winds
whispering waters
on a winter's marsh
the cry of geese flighting
the cry of children newly in the world

the cry of the hungry

sadness and joy
this is the music of the
living Earth

we cannot help but listen
recognising that this
is our music,
and the breath
which gives us life.

# Dinner at the Artist's house: Wilton Hill, Cumbria

Under the fell, the old farm is lit for us,
candles in every window, each guest drawn in,
enveloped in the warmth of welcome. The Artist,
breathing into life a corporeal presence,
makes this house a living work, the glow in corners
bringing joy to old stone, explosions of colour,
fabric, texture, form, the curve of blue in an old bowl;
swatches of colour rainbow-ing down the rooms,

Alive with love, this long table is laced with laughter,
friendship, an invisible web made visible.
We come here on brutal winter nights, through snow,
or now, when new lambs are in the fields,
this place a sanctuary where we are cherished,
celebrated by kindness, the spell the Artist weaves,
lingering, unforgotten.

# Meditation : Iona

Rain on the window; the quiet breathing of friends;
The candle burns.
By faith I know that outside this inner world
There is another, spreading out under rain,
Patterned in pools, secret among rocks.
Rain on lambs' backs as they shelter under flanks,
Rain in this slow light of time, as it has always been,
Wearing away stone, people and animals,
A battle with rain and wind and mind.
Rarely too little of it, coming after a bright day,
A reminder that this is the price to pay for living
In the Hebrides; this sulky slur of slow rain
Which will not lift, dark days which drive men to drink,
Days of mud brought to hearth,
Continuous trudging days of surviving in the wet,
Steamed-up windows, smoke blowing back
down chimneys, that sour stink of wet cloth,
the struggle recorded in the stone.

I'll lift my head from the rain's lashdown,
Throw back my hood, open my door
To the returning sun.

## Punamu ( greenstone) New Zealand

You are the green curve of the wave,
Lifting above an empty beach.
Frozen out of time, you are forever
Hurtling towards the white sand,
As the Maori canoes rise above the surf.

We are on the way. We are hunting.
The fish are in the water.
The Earth is our home.

This is the song of the punamu,
The chant which liquefies this greenstone
And gives it magic.  As it lies on my body,
Close, it takes its warmth from me.
In return, I am given protection, insight, dreams.
The Maori woman, Diana, standing in the marketplace,
Chose it for me.  If I am ever lost,
It has always called me home.

## Rose and Stone
IONA 2000

these are life forms
the rose petal and the stone

rose petal pliant in the wind
easily bruised
it dies after a day's life
delicately veined, its heart's colour

drawn into its centre
open to the universe
it scatters scented messages for the bee

the bee does not come to the stone

stones are hard, unyielding
if they give off scent
it is a distant air tang of the salt sea
in sun they hold heat

while petals wilt
beside me on the grass

our life is caught between them
the petal and the stone

stone..
not so short as a flower's life
not so long as almost eternity

days and nights and seasons
aeons and epochs
deep deep time

these mark the turning of the stone
on the sea's bed

a loving and a working
in the deep slow time of the world
turning, caressing,
the sea's fingers
on the seeming unchanging face of stone

until the sea finds
rest

stone stone,
pebble pebble
tiny grain of sand
sand to atom atom to proton,
into the secret heart of Creation

where God may be

so we turn and turn
the atoms of the world in the sea's hand
in the wind's hand in form and gravity
and fire
atom and atom
so we love and from our loving
from the drawing of the deep earth place
some god some creator
some mathematician
some star magician
draws down

the beginning
of the rose

## Unknown

One day I will set my boat
upon the sea's edge
and stepping into the cold water
I will launch myself
     Out There
where there are no boundaries

I know there is a great sea to cross
and in that wild country of waves
I may founder   certainly I will struggle
yet from that distant shore a scent of new things
comes back to me   some spice, some tang of strangeness

in this new country I may be happy
I may lie in a new bed in a strange room
And from the window in the morning
I may look over that same wild sea

in the distance
the outline of my old homeland will appear
mysterious upon the horizon

## Dawn Meditation : Himalaya

Dawn over the sacred lake
a boat is a dark crescent drifting
mist rolling up like silk
reveals reflections of mountains painted with fire

we can never hold these images
in the unmoving water
they melt away   the universe flows on
only for one breathless second it seemed
we were not transient beings
in a passing world
but held the stillness
in our hands

## Blowing Bubbles in the Nunnery gardens : Iona

Within the stone blocks of the old nunnery,
placed one on one, mortared with shells,
eddies and energies swirl without form.
But today we give life back to them,
an incandescence of rainbows, iridescence,
these globes of light, floating on the wind.
Joyful bubbles carry more than soap and breath
around old walls. Laughter, the love which comes from sharing,
visions of colour. Look how the wind takes them,
they are so light, and joy brings friendship, brings angels
into these cloisters, where window arches, catching sky,
must once have been fields of longing in those dark hours of chan
Better than the alternative – death in childbirth,
a brutal marriage; instead, toil, discipline, a denial of life's pleasur
but for that moment when the sun rises in the eastern sky,
and all is gold in the spaces of the walls.
Our globes of light go up like thoughts, up with the free wind,
invocations beyond those arched spaces where no nuns fly,
up with the heart, to where no cares remain.

## Midnight on Iona

Midnight hypnotises cats into slow walking.
Their eyes glittering in the half-moon,
they chirrup beside me. Puddles wink,
and one shrill shore bird squeals
like a bat in the dark.

The old, slow sea sighs onto sand, and back.
Mercury, quicksilver, is so silky around black rock
there seems no contact, no wetness, metal fingers
stroking a tune on the land. A sharp tune, a song,
sings the silent night to sleep with old tales,
as the moon goes behind a black cloud tower,
a whisper of orange diffused in the sky.

We know mountains are out there, beyond this little sea,
pale with snow, crofts where there is dreaming of tomorrow.
But for now, bats tumble and that solitary bird
cuts holes in the darkness with its call, and I am not afraid.
Walking alone under this luminous sky,
stars tremble over the sharp-cut nunnery,
its gable end black in the pale night.

All are sleeping but for a few yellow windows.
I am nearly there, nearly there at the point
where the world is turning, and yet is still.

## Sacred Earth

The humanity of Earth
is a woven part of our consciousness,
and of her Nature. Without us,
we would not 'know' that Earth is,
and Earth could not know herself.

She sees herself in our eyes
as beautiful. We stand
on the seashore and watch the waves
and know we are alive, and Earth through us
knows her aliveness. We know the morning
birdsong and the secret night,
and we give Earth back her treasures.

So life dreams itself
and we dream Earth in this unimaginable
Universe, where infinity waits for us
to find ourselves.

Maybe we are Earth's senses, cells
on her surface that tell her what she is like;
where trees are, ravines
and deep secret places,
white snows, eagle nests, flicking
rainbow fish in deep waters, how it feels
to walk barefoot on her rain-drenched grass.

We sing the song of Earth
with our everyday being. Be careful.
We are singing her dream back to her.
We may sing her to sleep, or death.

## Sacred Lake

Will the hibiscus flower and the marigold
Circle the sacred lake for ever?
The mountains are reflected in the water
Each a mirror of the other.
How do we know where one begins and the other ends?
Will the mountain come to the hibiscus flower,
Or the flower to the mountain?

## Happiness

Happiness

a new shaved field pale gold

crows lifting to the mountain

A bowl of old roses on the piano

Beethoven

## End of season: Iona

The pale sleeping morning stirs its stumps,
Hardly awake at half past eight.
Ben More stands proud above the Sound,
Capped with soft cloud in the morning's eye.
The scraping of the soul on wood
Is all the violin's response,
Echoing the wild ascetic's call to monkhood,
Solitude, the stone cell in winter, where man may see himself
Reflected. A hoodie pecks his image in the tractor mirror.
The crow, obsessed, punishes and scolds,
Perpetuating a cycle of vanity, deceit.
I'll turn away from this, find other lives,
An antidote to madness. That scrape of violins
Upon the soul exposes bone from flesh,
The shape and sense of us revealed.

## Manawatu Te Ra
*A Maori speaks for the World's tribe*


The word is in the wind. She hears it.
I do too, this Maori blessing on the day,
echoed in her rituals of grace,
her tobacco, the different coloured
cloths – the green, the white.
*Om mani padme hum*
Here too is the Jewel in the Heart of the Lotus,
here the Tibetan spins the prayer wheel,
Prayers, invocations. Fly up above the river
into the Great Sky. She is like the earth,
listening to trees, speaking in Earth's language;
the blessings of the day are written in her blood.
But something else. A move to spirit, to stand, listening:
*Manawatu te ra*. The Maori woman
stands in the heart of the day, her tribe
circling about her, protective, those ancestors
bringing wisdom to the wheel; the prayer wheel
for the Tibetan, the fastness of mountain.
Here the Maori weave flax into sacred pouches,
honouring punamu, holy jade, stone, Earth.

Dreams, death, birth.
Not only in the wind, but in the silence after,
the spirit wafts about us, singing tribal songs.

## Dawn on the River

It is dawn on the river.
Mist lies on the still surface like smoke.
We are travelling down to the estuary
to catch the tide. All other boats are asleep,
their portholes steamed with night breath,
cockpit doors shut, hatches fastened.

But we are free and new, beginning.
We are travelling down to the estuary,
we are going to the island, and over time
to the golden field. Here, the corn is not yet cut,
new light sits red gold on stalks; there is a misty sun
touching old elms, and one cottage with curtains closed,
dark around it, and dreams. But we are new and free,
beginning. Cows on the water's edge look up
as we pass, this strange object to puzzle them,
passing before their slow eyes.
Then, looking down to drink,
they let us go.

INDIGO DREAMS PUBLISHING
132 HINCKLEY ROAD
STONEY STANTON
LE9 4LN